CAPSULE STORIES

Masthead

Natasha Lioe, Founder and Publisher
Carolina VonKampen, Publisher and Editor in Chief
Stephanie Coley, Reader
Rhea Dhanbhoora, Reader
Hannah Fortna, Reader
Kendra Nuttall, Reader
Rachel Skelton, Reader
Deanne Sleet, Reader
Claire Taylor, Reader

Cover art by Darius Serebrova
Book design by Carolina VonKampen

Paperback ISBN: 978-1-953958-12-9
Ebook ISBN: 978-1-953958-13-6

CAPSULE STORIES

Spring 2022 Edition

Into the Light

Contents

Into the Light

For the first time in months, rays of sun fall through the window in the afternoon and land on your arms, warming you as you type on your keyboard. You look up to find the gray winter sky has been replaced with a hopeful blue, no clouds. Birdsong floats on the air. On a whim, you decide to go outside.

You find an empty bench in the park and sit, pull out the book you brought, and start reading. The sun envelops you, and suddenly it's too warm for your jacket. Moms with strollers and couples holding hands stroll past; from somewhere behind you, a boombox plays a song you almost recognize. You meet eyes with a guy sitting at a picnic table with a sketchbook, hand sweeping across the page. How can he even begin to capture the beauty of this day—the crocuses rising from the ground, the stained glass of an art installation coating the concrete in color, the earnestness of the trees trying on their green?

You feel elated. Lighter. You look around furtively before slipping off your shoes and setting your feet down into the grass for the first time since last summer. The earth squishes beneath your toes, so alive. The sun shines on your face and you know deep down that it will all be okay.

spring promises

Eileen Lynch

---

if winter's winds are harsh and biting,
then spring's are a loved one's gentle breaths
fanning against your face come morning.
lips brush skin, press to your forehead,
fingers push hair behind an ear,
clearing room to lean in and say:
the world is waking. you must too.
and she whispers of flowers blooming by the sill
while across the room the light spills,
warming the floorboards, the carpet, the sheets,
stirring whispers of life in the grass beyond the glass.
a promise: of the cold, coming undone,
and of the day that awaits you when eyes open
to once again greet the sun.

What Happens After the Snow Melts

Jessica Coles

---

when silence invites you, sit
with your spine against a lodgepole pine

let last year's dry grass smile into your fingertips
soil is busy with waiting for rain

gray sky knows how to say "I love you"
and always means it

there are so many languages
too wide for your unstretched mouth

they rest like cloud-wisps tucked
under a magpie's tongue for safekeeping

adapt your organs
to this kind of listening

this sky-earth hum your body
channels and disrupts

Vernal Invocation

Jessica Coles

Walk the curved roads of this traffic-calmed neighborhood.
Stop in a small park that is remembering green.
Stay where the quiet words tell you to close your eyes.
Let new grass rustle against the smallest muscles in your feet.

Picture strangers looking out their windows
from this cluster of houses. You have become your strangeness,
roots are waking up. Introduce yourself to the sun
as a mystic, a magician, a deeply unsettling sorceress.

Tell it that the ravens know your name, that the soil sings
when you wriggle your toes. Call down the sky
to paint your lips cloud-silver. This is the route home
you've been waiting for. Your ankle bones

jangle a tune, anticipate renewal in the love you tuck
between your soles and the last stubborn granules of snow.

Signs

Jessica Coles

I know it's spring because
I'm on my knees in the front yard
checking for crocus shoots
in the dead grass
around the weeping birch

teaching my daughter to tell the difference
between these clusters of green and the solitary
spikes of new grass, though I'm not sure
who taught me, though someone
must have said: this is how you will know

when something new is growing, this is how you trust
what flowers will follow, this is how time takes
back what it gives, but it gives again
in so many ways I learn this from soil
and that from thatch until I

trust my intuition of which green to attend
find fresh sprouts amid senescence
exactly where I planted it:

her shining eyes, a response to my sunshine

a fragile okay

Jessica Coles

I'm not wrong to love the most
urgent things today: clear blue sky
sunscreen-scented hands

hungry bees sip a moment of

uneven peace, unsent texts
to dead relatives, numb balance
of anxiety and relief. Memories

percolate in ephemeral sunshine
persistent as dandelions at the edge
of the school. These early bees cross-pollinate

old/new loves, collect nectar from
mistaken flowers, silken sweet
opportunities to fail

Tuesday, Taking on Water

Virginia Laurie

I'd forgotten about the hole in the bottom of my white sneakers until I had to walk a quarter mile in the rain, a mean rain too— Not a wild shower that makes me feel half wolf and savagely clean, thoroughly, cathartically run through, out on the press felts and pushed until there is nothing left but a midnight black imprint of myself on the ground. Not that. Just a mean drizzle, unrelenting and defining the word dreary. Just enough to soak my right sock, because, like I said, there's a hole there—and the depression is like that sometimes.

I forget there's a little hole—just a crack, really—in the rubber gray matter where water can slip in. I'm well aware of it now, the feel of it, the saturation, but I'll forget again and soon. I'll wear my white sneakers into a deluge then remember how cheap they are and shipwrecked.

So, the depression. It catches me off guard sometimes.

I suppose that's progress, to forget long enough to be surprised every month, like a period.
You think, How could I have forgotten? And then you forget. It helps that you want to forget.
I don't want to remember the bad days, don't want to feel my toes squelch, know my tennis shoes will smell like mildew later. That if I get new ones, I'll have to break them in again.

My parents would tell me to just buy new shoes. The same ones even, if I know where they're sold, and I do: the Walmart off Lee Highway. They worked hard so I wouldn't have to pinch my own pennies, and I know this. That's not the point.

The point is, I like these shoes, and I don't want to fix everything.
I like things a bit rough at the edges, stray ink and walking on
a waterbed.

Generally, I like rust. I like maximalism and sloppiness. I
like faded hair dye and chipped nail polish, dusty frames,
half-melted pocket candy, and unused stickers. I like, some-
times, how fragile the world makes me, how easy it is to let it
in. It's better than the numbness,
which is its own kind of drowning.

I can live a bit waterlogged, up to the neck. I'm a pretty good
swimmer.

When I swim real fast, my lungs heave with it, and my limbs
prickle with citrus,
which makes me smile, even while I'm still heaving.

Now, the only thing swimming is my right foot. I am no lon-
ger thinking about depression, but of rivers and lakes. I love
water. This is okay. The feeling is repulsive, a bit queasy, but
it is okay.

I take the long way, because I like the view. It's still raining. It
is okay. We will get dinner later. The cats will knock my shins
until I feed them. I will read another book for class, which is
okay. We will probably eat on the couch again, maybe cut on
music, something in another language.

It is okay.

My sock will dry, and soon.

It is okay.

Early

Luciana Francis

The sky has cleared
like a sea parted by faith,

and it feels like the first morning.
We saw it coming,

we've pushed through—
the storm before the calm.

Morning light paints a picture
as I draw the curtains—

newborn dawn, as smooth
as a pebble. The sun bares its crown

look what we found!
on the other side of the weather.

yarn

Luciana Francis

birdsong
her face in the mirror
she turns toward the window
as the morning light lingers
in a quiet neighborhood
surrounded by fields
with her finger she draws
a peak and the path
that will take her there
unwound yarn in scarlet red
and she already knows
what she'll wear

To Lose

Veronica Nation

The charge of daylight brings morning.
From the unmoving dust, I see time,
which has passed and settled and set
quietly on my shelves. My books are well-
read and yellowed, the color of leaves
fallen in the backyard, left to rest.

I feel the weight of unrest
heavy in my body. I am mourning
the brightness of my brother's eyes. It relieves
some sort of constricted breath, and time
moves slowly in this action. I am unwell,
I think. I am unable to breathe and reset.

I see everything in black and white. The upset
of death lingers. I think, what was the rest
of his life going to be? I let myself dwell
on images in my head of my brother in the morning,
eating chicken wings for breakfast, not a care of time
or deadlines. Greasy fingers, watching the leaves.

Every poem I write reminds me that he leaves.
Each memory of him dissipates. I do not set
realistic expectations of myself with time—
that is to say, I do not let myself rest
after experiencing loss. I wake up in the morning
and go to work as if all has been well.

The day after my brother died, I said a farewell
not to him or to his body, but to the long-sleeve

navy sweater I bought him for winter. I am not mourning
clothing, but rather the fact that he will never set
foot again in his room of rest.
I think of what he could have been all the time.

And the dust of my shelves, the reminder of time
is not so easy to forgive. I have done well
to stay still yet ambitious, to rest
but to prosper. I wonder what this leaves
me: an understanding of death, of the asset
that is life, or the thanks for the morning?

I do thank the morning for its sun. I thank time for its passing.
I weave love so well into my life. I set up my bookshelves with
color-coded intention. Hide leaves in the pages of my journal. I rest.

I do thank the morning for its sun.

Release

Veronica Nation

The nights were cold, the crack in my window
packed with towels to absorb the chill.
I saw you in a dream, something like a sign
telling me you were okay, not drowning
like my mind suggested you might be.
*

The buds were starting to sprout
so late this year I thought we would
never have dandelion heads to blow on,
cattails to split open, petals to pick off our shoulders
and use as ornaments for our hair.
*

A warmth moved me, a warmth unfelt in the fall.
You told me, in a dream, to listen to cicadas,
to count the time with crickets, to keep
the front porch light on for the kids
whose parents wouldn't know they had snuck out
to smoke and stargaze and kiss the spring hello.

False Spring

Sara Davis

Imagine having something good simply because you want it. Imagine there is not a cloud in the sky, and just for today the sunlight is so warm you can almost see it, soft and gold. And when you take off your cardigan you can feel the light spreading on your skin, as sugar coats the tongue. And you're walking to meet a friend, and you're on time for a change, and your chatter flows like cream, no gaps. And there are no leaves on the trees yet so it's just sunlight and the warmth tentatively rising from the sidewalk the whole way. Imagine the effervescence you suddenly feel is not the simple chemistry of caffeine plus companionship plus exercise—your neurons are practically snapping with glee, walking has been a grim business this winter—but the natural order of things reasserting itself, a seasonal shift. And your laughter catches a little on the way out, you're a little rusty, but the pair of you can't seem to stop making jokes, are you always this witty or are you just warm enough for the first time your skin can remember? You keep taking little sips of it all, even through the cotton of your mask it feels like a new beginning, you want to inhale it all in so that your whole body lights up but don't rush, go slow, it's gone so fast.

Slow Rise

Jeremy Chu

The window unlatched, where
daybreak pummeled itself through
studio window time again:

a spotless window,
a forgetful bird.

I felt the thickest bones of it
wrestle its way past the
morning swell of faces,
thrashing its limbs caught
between the thick vinework
of furniture, its great light parts
splayed throughout the landscape
of bedframe and bookshelf.

The dense body settled
when its breathing slowed
to one terminal exhale, and so
the day was had.

It could be seen across the far
continents of city blocks:

wherever the window
was found, so too was
the bird of morning,
forgetting.

Suncatcher

Hantian Zhang

The sun has come in through the light well. It cuts a geometric patch on the wall, darkening the flower shop's un-lit dimensions by contrast. Carla pauses what she has been doing—sorting out the fresh bunches just brought in from the wholesale—and stares at the dappled pattern inside this patch, motes of shades resembling broken parallels. She understands them as the effect of uneven glass, a slab probably as old as the Victorian that houses the shop; she thinks about possible elements to complement it: colors, shapes, and textures.

She visits issues like this often, since she came to San Francisco to study making stained glass, since enough commissions had given her the confidence for her own product line. She rented an artist studio in Dogpatch and set up a website, just when Julie needed to go back to St. Louis to attend her ailing parents. She and Julie go way back, besties in high school and reconnected two years ago, after college and first jobs. She told Julie she'd look after her shop, even without being offered a small corner for her glasswork. Part of her hoped to work here, actually, comfortably alone and inspired by all those colors. And now, the dappled pattern does inspire a new design, a left half-moon of emerald mirroring a right half, stripes cut from a slab that casts dapples, interlaced with clear pink and light rutilant.

Her hands are still sorting the flowers, but her mind is assembling the pieces, rearranging them for better effects just when the shopkeeper's bell rings. She looks up to greet the first customer of the day, a middle-aged woman who nods back but then passes her, not finding what she has been looking for and then walking straight out. Carla returns to sorting the flowers but lets out a sigh, so slightly that she barely notices it. Most customers are like that. The flower business hardly breaks even, and her stained glass seldom sells here. The shop duties also push her glassmaking to before nine or after seven, or Mondays when the shop is closed. She has to remind herself the arrangement is only temporary, and there's comfort in doing all this for her friend. Even though she has been wearing the loner hat for as long as she remembers, she has, at least, this one friend she could carve out a part of herself for.

The next customer buys a potted fern without saying a word, and the one after pulls out one bouquet after another without purchasing any of them. When the fourth walks in soon after, Carla is still tidying up the disarray the previous customer has just left. Only the swishing sound of the plastic wrapper in the register's direction prompts her to stand up.

The customer is already waiting with a bouquet of lilies. He is a sandy-haired white man about fifty, lines on the face roughly resemble her own father's. His eyes brighten up when they meet the suncatchers on the wall.

"These look familiar." He has a fast cadence of speech. "Are they from Carla Woo Studio?"

Once in a while, Carla would get a chummier-than-usual customer, but what is the chance of running into someone impressed by your work like this, in this anonymous city, in this enormous world? "Yes, I made them," she says, a flash of surprise widening her eyes.

"So you are the artist." The man lowers his bouquet. "I've ordered pieces from you before, and my daughter loves them—she could literally sit in front of a piece and follow the movement of the shades for hours. One of our orders was big, with orange and purple half-moons and bubbles." He gestures, demonstrating the shape and size.

"Oh, that's Dazzle and Razzle." Carla smiles. "I had this idea of creating a suncatcher larger than usual—to catch more sun, of course."

"I didn't know you have a shop," he says, extending his credit card for the flowers.

"I sell online, mostly," Carla says, plugging the Square card reader into her phone, "but my studio is elsewhere. I'm now helping my friend here, and she allows me to sell my work for free."

"Nice," he says as she swipes his card. "Actually, I visited your website weeks ago. Everything was marked Sold Out, though, so I wondered whether you were out of business."

"Oh." Carla chuckles. "No, I'm getting by. The work here takes lots of time, so now I work on my glass in the evenings and on Mondays. I mark Sold Out to block out new orders, so I get to take only as much work as I can handle."

"I see," the man says. He picks up his bouquet and tilts his body, appearing ready to leave but then pauses. "You see, Carla, I want to ask you a favor. I'm Matt, by the way."

"Yes?" she says as she shakes his extended hand.

"You said you work on your stained glass on Mondays?"

"Yes?"

"Can I take my daughter to visit your studio, like tomorrow?"

"Err." Carla is unsure. While she enjoys Matt's interest in her work, and the thought that this might lead to sales does skitter across her mind, she feels the potential of duplicity is clouding her ability to see through the unusual request. Her habit is to retreat from strangers; her inclination is to guard her alone time.

"You see, this is just for my daughter." Matt takes a step closer. "She is nine. I've never seen her so obsessed with an object more than your suncatcher. She's been asking me how to make one, and she'll be thrilled if she could learn that from you. We'll be in and out, I promise."

His head tilts when he says all this, the furrows on his forehead show. Carla has never expected her work to have such an impact. She withholds questions like *don't you have to work tomorrow* and *where's the mother* and looks up at Matt. There is no way to see through him, of course; she can only decide that he does look like a father taking an opportunity, even just a stumped-upon one, to put a smile on his daughter's face. Carla's own father seldom gave her presents; growing up, she wondered whether her biological parents would do that—but why, then, had they given her up?

"Okay," Carla says, softening her tone before thinking it through, "how about 9 a.m. tomorrow?"

"Wonderful," Matt says, "thank you so much."

"Do you want me to write down the address?"

"Please."

That evening, Carla gets a call from Julie. She asks about her updates in Missouri, then mentions that a customer had requested to visit her studio because his daughter is a fan.

"That's wonderful," Julie says, "to meet someone so appreciating your work."

"But you know me," Carla says. "I'd prefer to keep that time all to myself."

"Consider it marketing time, necessary for any business."

"Thus says the salesgirl-turned-florist."

"Thus says the loner-turned-artist."

Monday morning, Carla arrives at the studio at 7 a.m., and works nonstop till the appointed time. She steps to the window and looks down, eyes following a sedan with a large scratch on the rear door. It pulls over across the street, and Matt and his little girl emerge from there.

So there is really a daughter, then. She walks down and into the sun. Matt sees her and waves. His girl is thin and weary-looking, head covered with an unseasonal wool beanie, eyes Asian and casting down. She looks even younger than nine.

Carla waves back and fixes her eyes on the girl, her thoughts vacillating between Asian wife and adoptee. She smiles at her as they cross the street, but the girl keeps her eyes down until the last, when Matt and Carla are already exchanging greetings. She bites into her lower lip and steals a glance, a flash withdrawn so quickly that Carla almost misses it.

"I'm Carla. What's your name?" She bows down and extends her hand. The girl doesn't take it; she purses her lips and takes a step back as if startled.

"Her name is Jenny," Matt answers for her. "We chose a name that sounds like her Korean name, Jeong, meaning 'pure,' the agency told us."

An adoptee like me, then, Carla thinks as she straightens her back. An emotion, lighter than sadness and shallower than communion, holds her, and in that, she decides to let the girl keep her distance. She turns, leads the way through the steep staircases and the dingy corridors. She opens the door to her studio, a corner space now flooded with the morning sun. She is about to lead them on to her working station by the windowsill, her paraphernalia on the nearby shelves, but a look at her guests tells her that none is more attention-grabbing than the suncatchers hanging on the window: all the sunrays being held there, all the shades and shapes they cast on the floor. The awe on their faces reminds her of her own being surrounded by such an abundance of color for the first time, in Seattle's Gethsemane Church when she visited Julie almost ten years ago.

"Those are the finished commissions for this month. I haven't shipped them out yet," she explains and only then thinks of the etiquette of being a host. "Do you need some water?" She apologizes, "I'm not used to having visitors, so there's only one mug. Hope you don't mind drinking from it in turn?"

Matt thanks her, for himself and then looks down to check for Jenny. But the girl is not by him already. Dropping her father's hand, she is walking into the middle of the room. She raises her hands amid the colors, palms to eye level as if holding up something of weight. She moves within the colored shadows but keeps her hands upraised, examining the colors so intently as if she can tell them apart simply by feeling, orange's and purple's effects different on her skin.

Synesthesia, the word comes to Carla. *Could colors have a synesthetic effect?* she thinks as she steps into the colored shades herself, taking in the blue tinge of the sky and feeling the sun's warmth. It calms her, much more so than usual, and in that warmth and calm, she thinks it might not be so bizarre an idea that colors can be tactile.

"Which color is your favorite?" she walks up to the girl's side and asks; she appreciates the thought she has inspired in her.

"Red," Jenny says, her eyes meeting Carla's for the first time, her voice small but clear.

"Why?"

"It makes me warm," Jenny says, "like when I'm at school, with many people."

For a moment, Carla recalls her own being with many people, how it was just her and Julie sitting together at their high school's cafeteria, or later, when they attended colleges in different cities, how it was just her at the end row of the lecture hall. Even at the stained glass workshop attended by less than ten people, Carla still preferred staying at the edge of the circle. She reasoned that that helped her to concentrate, from a distance, undisturbed.

"Do you like to be with many people?" she asks kindly.

"I sometimes do, but don't when they laugh at me."

About what? Jenny's eyes are already downcast. Carla looks up to Matt, the moment when his murmur "alopecia" reaches her ears. She does not understand but knows kids could be picked on for all kinds of puerilities, as she knows the beanie summarizes once and for all the laugh's effect. She herself was laughed at once, at a neighbor kid's birthday party for looking different from her parents, the McDougalls. Her preference for being alone probably started around then, and the people around her all got that signal and let her. Julie was a "loner," too, for being biracial, or whatever other trivial reasons that appeared colossal.

"Come here." She leans down toward the girl. "I'll show you how to make a suncatcher." She pictures Jenny losing herself to the suncatchers as a solace, the room's layout and furniture all fuzzy but the suncatchers as real as the ones before them, the same colors being held in the glass, the same rhythm of their changing as the sun's position shifts.

"Afterward, she can take it as my gift," she says as she turns to Matt.

"That would be unnecessary," Matt says hurriedly, "I mean, I can definitely pay you."

"No, my pleasure," Carla says, "just a small suncatcher. You know, I'm an adoptee from China myself."

"You are?" Matt says. Jenny also looks up to her.

"Yes," Carla says, unsure why she has brought it up. She evades Matt's eyes and steps to her cabin, where she keeps her design sketches and glass slabs. "In Missouri. Growing up, I always knew I was different; maybe that's why I don't have many friends."

"People here don't seem to exclude her for being adopted," Matt whispers, "but she has clumps of hair falling out. We've been treating her, but those other kids—you can't imagine."

Maybe there's more that she doesn't tell? Carla wonders but decides not to ask. Once, in the junior year of high school, Julie was spit at on her way home, but Julie never told this to her parents. Further back in middle school, though, Julie did report the names she had been called. Carla goes through her binder of design sketches and wonders why she herself was not called such names—or they were blotted out by her memory for good? All this happened ten, fifteen years ago, when Missouri was a different kind of place. Now, on this spring day and in this colorful room, such memories feel remote and ungrounded, made up by her own mind.

She picks a design and returns to the workstation with the needed glass. She flashes a smile at Jenny as kindly as she can. "Now, we can begin to make you a suncatcher."

The girl does not cheer or even smile, but she walks up to Carla, hands up on the workstation's rim, and eyes upon her. And it is in her stare that Carla puts the design sketch under the glass, readying to draw the shapes according to her blueprint. It is Starburst, the design she had conceived only yesterday morning, right before Matt's visit. She sketched it only last night. In its current form, the round shape makes it a time-consuming piece compared to squares or triangles, but somehow Carla is keen on making it for the girl. She would have smiled if someone had given her such a gift.

"The first step of making a suncatcher is to design it," she explains as she readies her markers. "But in our case, we use a ready design. Now I am drawing the design on the glass. Look, it is a moon, with halves made from different kinds of glass."

The girl nods, smiling faintly. Even now, with the mid-morning sun heating up the air, she still does not take off her beanie. Carla shifts her attention back to the drawing until she finishes. "I'm going to cut the glass now," she says as her eyes shift between Matt's and Jenny's, "and it is important to protect your eyes against the shards that might fly off. I have only one pair of goggles, so I need you to step far away from me."

She moves about in the space created by their retreat, holding the glasscutter like a pen, making furrows on the glass along the lines she had drawn earlier. The squeal that the glasscutter makes leads Jenny to raise her hands again, stuffing her index fingers into her ears. But her eyes still shine, her attention is still keen. Carla then pulls out a plier, a tool that looks like a pair of thick, black chopsticks hinged at the middle. She applies the plier on the furrow and gives it a press, and Jenny laughs aloud when the glass cracks along the line, easily and almost right to the shape that Carla had drawn.

Carla smiles at Jenny's laughter, recalling her own first impression when she saw a piece of glass broken just like that, in her workshop instructor's hands, and making the same crisp sound. Even for a loner, there are still joyful moments. She uses a smaller plier to fine-tune the glass cutouts into her desired shapes, then signals her guests to come back closer.

"Now we are at the next step, foiling." She points to her caddy that holds five threads of foils of different widths, all made of copper and rolled up like duct tapes. She dusts off the glass pieces one by one, pulls out a thread, and cuts and crimps it along the edge of the glass. She allows Jenny to touch when she finishes, and then assigns her the job to place them together like the design commands.

She glances at the time: almost eleven. She declares they are now at the next and to her the most exciting step: joining the pieces together. She plugs in the fat pen-like soldering iron, applying its burning tip to melt the solder wire into a semiliquid, which she then uses to fill the gaps between the glass pieces. She wears a glove because there is lead in the solder, but she tells Matt and Jenny that they should be fine if they refrain from touching it. To further minimize the impact, she turns on the smoke absorber; she opens the window to let in the fresh air.

"Why don't we just use glue?" Jenny asks, after all the bother Carla had to go through.

Carla pauses her movements, searching in her mind for an answer that is not there. "I don't know," she can only admit. "Can I Google it after we are finished?"

"Okay." Jenny nods and smiles.

And that smile delights her—the broadest of the day, almost amazing in that you can smile at such a plain and mundane answer, not apparently smile-inducing in any manner. Carla is suddenly aware of the additional care she now puts into the piece as she finishes up her polishing, the sense of accomplishment when it is done. "Shall we put it up on the window," she asks Jenny, "to make it dry faster, and to see its effect against the sun?"

"Yeah!" the girl yelps cheerfully.

"It's yours now," Carla says as she hangs the suncatcher up. "It's my gift for you."

"And what would you say to that, Jenny?" Matt now jumps in, in a tender tone.

"Thank you," Jenny says, her words melt into another broad smile as she looks away, looking shy or even embarrassed.

The three of them take a step back, looking up to all the suncatchers, the newest Starburst, the accumulation of a whole month's orders. The sun is already too high to cast colorful shadows on the floor, but against the endless sky, all the colors held in the suncatchers have shifted, moving toward the blue end of the spectrum. Squinting a little, you can see the largest bubbles in pieces containing hand-rolled glass, the grains of its unevenness.

"Oh, you are so charming," Carla says.

"What?" Matt looks at her.

"Yes?"

"You were saying?"

"Oh," Carla chuckles as she responds. "I must have been talking to the suncatchers—I sometimes do talk to them."

"Me, too," Jenny interjects, "I make wishes to my suncatchers all the time, and they tell me all are safe with them."

"You are just like me, then," Carla says, moving closer to the girl and giving her shoulder a tender pat. "We have more friends than we've ever realized."

The Need
for New
Words

Andrew J. Calis

I'm not going to say *diversity* is like a stained
glass window (though it is) because
that prismatic light, that light that swims
in waves too wide for sight, seems unreal.

It only lives in chapels; but I've seen
faces live in wild freedom
in the world—the world which welcomes difference,
sometimes. Not often.

We rely
on each other now. We rely
on ourselves. We make families
and watch them—melding selves into

themselves. We've spent the wealth of friendship,
rested in our riches, in the ways
we speak when no one speaks for us, our words
our own, a flock of voices soaring up

and up filling up the sky like stars
widening their reach like arms; each light
shimmering like gold, this light we make,
that only we could make—it looks a lot

like love, doesn't it? It looks
a lot like love.

Shine

Andrew J. Calis

It's hard to blind
when you aren't
of the sun.

Born brown, before I knew
what brown was, I found
out, learned what I was,

learned to love the yellow glow
of sand, wide-spreading over
my past—my dad
born in Jerusalem,

kept out of the city
by yellowed walls,
left with sand
that stained his skin
and hardened it.

Yellow sand that stings
my eyes when I think
about his past, that clouds
the air, that buries like a shroud
his history and keeps it warm,
alive. There's him

in me—I see it like a ghost
when
there are
no words;

---

then
I'm broken open
like the earth in flower,

and suddenly I breathe
the air, I glow,
I shine like light.

I shine like light

Arriving at School First

Andrew J. Calis

The silence of the morning arrives before
we do. It stills the air. It forces out
the rush of yesterday. The silence sits
in my room, fills it—a painful mix
of apathy, and sloth. It chafes like grout
on my skin.

       Then into this mess of morning pours

the sound of someone coming down the hall—
walls rebounding the sound now, the unspoken credo
of new life here, of some breath to stir
the noiselessness to music; the gossamer
hope that this day brings another need:
voices rich with laughter, bent with all
this uncontained new joy. Like light,
it layers out; it warms; it thrills;
old visions animated with new sight,
it overflows its home. It will not stay
itself. It lives and lives and see the way
it echoes joy, how it will not hold still?

An Ear to the Ground

Andrew J. Calis

We see before we hear the thunder, and cannot
hear the rumble of tectonic plates
until too late, when stones are brought like teeth
from dead earth. On what large infinity
we live. And still, Earth sinks into the wider
plane. A raindrop dropped into the sea.
Listen closely, with just your heels, and
you might see the unforgotten start:
the sun that rose after days of rain,
and how it made the almost cloudless sky
grow over the Shenandoah mountains,
and then more than ever feel how small
we are, and how large.

Rinse and Wring

Matthew Miller

Gloss on lines from "Spring" by Gerard Manley Hopkins

Nothing is so beautiful as Spring –
When weeds, in wheels, shoot long and lovely and lush;
Thrush's eggs look little low heavens, and thrush
Through the echoing timber does so rinse and wring . . .

Bright on east slopes of Shenandoah,
April sun splits sugar maple and white ash.
Redbuds like scribbles, racing past windows
as our van traces the brown mountain's spine.
It is slowly greening, grass lining the passes,
daffodils freckling the forest's face.
Daughter of the stars, washing winter away
down her bare arms, in waterfalls that bloom
in splashes like clear florets opening.
Nothing is so beautiful as spring.

We turn our eyes to the clouds behind
and whisper gratitude. We tie tight loops
in hiking boots. Ankles and attitudes
can turn swiftly in our scree-strewn descents
to the river's start. Boulders tumble down-
stream, like clods turned up plowing the garden.
My children hop rock to rock, like migrant
birds bustling between branches. A warbler
pecks for insects along the mossy rush
when weeds, in wheels, shoot long and lovely and lush.

Sunlit stones make home for salamander
and ribbon snake, slipping into grottoes
unseen. They sip air fresh and muddy,
knowing rain often rides the next horizon.
Lowering myself around the switchbacks,
search rotten leaves for gifts, geraniums
or maidenhair fern. Smoke from controlled burns
obscures northwestern rims, so I cannot
look to future sunsets. On the hillside,
thrush's eggs look little low heavens, and thrush

harmonize with water drops and the crunch
of our feet on the path of this hollow.
Walking sticks click over talus cliffs that rise
from the chestnut. Scarlet tanagers flash
by oaks, roving skies for moth and sawflies.
There's so much I can name, but not explain,
like why there is so much that has to die
for spring to feel this alive. But my kids
just pray for everything. Their simple voice
through the echoing timber does so rinse and wring.

for spring to feel
this alive

Take Pleasure

V. Bray

Take pleasure in the small things,
Buddha instructs.

You shine in predawn darkness,
an edge of anticipation,
seeking companionship
seeking warmth.

I lean into your triangle face
greeting me
as the sun rises
and sleep has not yet
left my eyes.

With a deep chortle-like purr
you push your white and ginger patches,
short-haired and sleek,
against my hand.

There is nothing mundane
about peace.

Revise

V. Bray

I lost my home when you died
leaving the taste
      of steaming red sauce,
      sautéed cabbage,
      and homemade mashed potatoes
lingering on my tongue.

All your gratitude filled my pit of need
      "Thank you, thank you, my angel."
      "I love you most of all."

In your empty house I vacuum up
fallen identities
      caregiver,
      granddaughter,
      gospodynka.

I try to build a new way to be.

Revise, revise, revise.

But I am not handy.
      I do not know how to rebuild.

In my mind I hear you say,
      "Go, talk to the trees."

The grove of old sycamores waits.

I Go to Oaks for Answers

Annie Powell Stone

If I hurry I can catch
the golden hour kissing
the sun side of their trunks,
ridged bark aglow
while the shadow side cools
with darkening sky.

      "How?" I ask, always pressing process,
      "With time," the oaks reply.

I trace the barred owl's call
to his nest, tucked amongst new leaves,
with its penthouse view.
He is headed out for the evening,
riding sweet breeze, perhaps the same
one that will follow me home.

      "Who?" I ask, an owl's echo,
      "You," the oaks reply.

I go searching for my inner child
and find her, again, swinging from the branches
of an oak we used to have and used to love.
Gone now--- from here at least---
they have chosen to stay together
in Rumi's field.

      "Why?" I ask, the perennial childhood query,
      "Because life," the oaks reply.

The campus bells chime the hour
and I watch a woman stop and listen, counting,
because she actually does not know the time.
And I am inspired by a life like that,
one that reads years in trunk rings
or counts seasons by the stars.

with time

standing on hair's end

Annie Powell Stone

why is it I feel I can't wait
when that is what a spider does
all day
(upside down, no less)
with eight legs and eggs
to hatch
surely she has a lot to do, too,
always some corner to patch

but she knows:
there is only so much
web you can weave
and then it is time
to let minutes pass
without spinning,
to let the sun move across the sky
without you pulling it on a string.

here a dandelion seed is caught
in her threads
like an open umbrella
delivered to a tree on a storm,
a small wish waiting.
her green and orange stripes shine,
blue legs resting
but ready.

Paper Stars

Annie Powell Stone

He jumps on the canvas hump
of the living room chair
telling me he wants to see the world.
From atop the creaking spring dromedary
he sings his bouncing rocket ship travel plans
as they constellate on the drywall sky.

Caravans of sippy cups and socks
pad down our hallway where floorboard gaps
are exciting chasms into secret realms.
His finger trails castle tops, snow drops,
and stops
at the sound of a new word.

Amidst the moving dapple shade
of a tree kissed by breeze
the challenge of a new bike awaits.
There are bugs to investigate
and ship sails to fill with puffed cheeks
on this wandering neighborhood day.

Back in the Sun Again

Simone Woods

My eyes are drawn to a movement occurring somewhere outside the window. I glance out and spot the change: the lady who lives in the apartment building across from ours has ventured out onto her balcony, as she does multiple times a day. I pause, staring as I place my hand against my brow casting a little shadow over my eyes. She leans her long arms out against the rail and gazes onto the parking lot. Her white hair is fixed into a tightly wound bun as usual, but I notice something different about her. Her winter outfit, the one that I've seen her wear these past few months—composed completely of black, apron around her waist, sleeves rolled up carefully—has morphed into a lighter, brighter ensemble. I am somewhat shocked at how different she now looks with her soft knit pink jumper; even her hair, although the style unchanged, looks a little less severe. I can't quite make it out, but I can glimpse a certain gentleness to her face that I've never recognized before. She smiles at some kids rolling around on scooters on the concrete and, just before she turns to look in my direction, I move my gaze away from the window.

I bustle around the lounge room, making big lurching steps to pick up my phone laying on the armrest of our IKEA couch, and then out into the hallway. Bruno is sitting ready in the pram and, although he's a calm and happy baby with a seemingly endless well of patience, he's still only a one-year-old and I'm aware that I could be met with squawks or cries at any moment. I smile at him and tap his nose as I reach down to grab my boots from the floor. His legs and socked feet are kicking about, free; the weather is finally warm enough that we don't need his great big cocooning foot muff for the pram anymore. I see the rays of sun on the wooden floor of Zsolt's room, sprinkled with bouncy balls, LEGOs, and other odds and ends as usual, and decide that it's safe enough to even wear suede boots—such a treat. I don't need a scarf either, so I'm ready in two minutes instead of ten; it's so easy to leave the apartment now—without all the winter layers, without the pain, and without the fear.

We take a walk every day after lunch, Bruno and I—well, I walk while he's strapped into the pram, sucking on his index finger, gradually finding his way into sleep. These walks have become more than a routine; they are a ritual. They keep reminding me that life can go on, that there is life and laughter and brightness all around now. The weather is getting slightly warmer; I've noticed that these past few days, and I am fairly certain that we won't have any more snow this year—not even the freak April snow that native Germans tell me is always possible, even after a period of warmth. Today there is a glow in the air that carries the memory of summer, the hope and the faith that it will arrive once again.

I notice little glints of purple in the grass; the crocus bulbs have obviously felt secure enough with this warmth to break through the earth. I think back to the version of these walks that we took this time last year—that dark and grim year when even though there was physical light, I could barely make it out. Those walks had made me feel weighed down: I would have Bruno strapped to my chest in the Ergobaby carrier and Zsolt would ride alongside us on his trike. This was after he'd stopped asking when he was going to see his daycare friends again; even as a mere two-and-a-half-year-old, he had known that the long pauses and unsatisfactory answers that Hugo and I responded with meant bad news. We had needed to carve some structure into those days that felt like one unending, connected stream, and Hugo needed to work, so, every day we walked and walked and walked. I would try to stretch out those neighborhood walks so that they would swell to fill the whole morning. Even though the walks had taken me out of our apartment—that we, having become a family of four, were now brimming out of—and into the expanse of outside, I had felt trapped like I was on some kind of spinning wheel that I couldn't find a way to exit. Having a baby a couple of weeks before the world turned upside down had turned out to be very bad timing indeed. Those walks, laden with Bruno, had induced peculiar aches in my pelvis. Each day I would walk, seemingly chatting with Zsolt while Bruno dozed, but my mind would be stuck somewhere deep inside my body, worrying about all its unanticipated aches and new strange quirks, wondering if I would ever feel at home in my own body again, whether I would ever feel like myself again.

Today, as I have for the easily remembered past, I am walking briskly, because I like to walk fast, to feel how freely and easily my body can now move—now that the pains have faded like the color of clothing left out in the sun too many times; now that my body is not weighed down by carrying a baby who ate well and gained fat rolls by the week. Zsolt is not with us now either; he's happily back at daycare—now hopefully on his final return, after being in and out, with the last out expanding to seven whole months over winter. There had been a glimmer of reprieve last summer (as if Europe itself had breathed a sigh of relief), but then winter brought us to greater depths of despair. I didn't think it would be possible for them to keep everything shut up for that long, but they did. It was worse than the first lockdown, because we had grown to believe over the summer that it was over, but no, it was only the beginning. A lot happened over last winter: Zsolt lost a tooth (from an unfortunate accident), I spent days, weeks, months in a depressive time warp where I began to feel like nothing mattered anymore. The winter—normally welcomingly refreshing in its cold and quiet—was oppressive this time; I often felt my chest tightening, barring the air from fully reaching my lungs. But it was during this time as we walked around in the snow as the light quickly faded, and as the Christmas lights glittered, that I began concocting little warm plans in my mind, on the way to finding myself again. Or, perhaps, to finding a new me.

Some days, Bruno and I go to the bakery. I usually buy myself a chunky slice of heavy German plum streusel cake and a brezen for Bruno. But I peer over the pram today and see his dark eyelashes are intertwined and his finger has dropped from his mouth, leaving a little O-shaped opening. I decide instead to take a place on a sunny park bench. I watch as people move about: mothers, like me, strolling along pushing prams of various shapes and sizes, old people snailing along cautiously with their walking frames, groups of tweens kicking around soccer balls or playing badminton. I feel relaxed even though there is a lot of noise: laughter, excited yells and yelps, the occasional bark of a dog—the world feels like it's moving again, bustling even, and I am glad to be out here soaking up the sun and the hope. There is life again.

When we arrive home, Bruno naps. Unlike his older brother who seemingly didn't sleep for longer than two hours ever in the first eighteen months of his life, Bruno is the ultimate sleeper: I won't hear a peep from him for the next three hours, four even. This gives me plenty of time to write. I sit in the armchair, my new writing home, prop my legs up on the footstool, enjoying the nakedness of my feet on the fabric, balance my laptop somewhat precariously on a cushion on my lap, and then I let the words flow out. It is hard to imagine that there was ever a time when I didn't write, when this wasn't at all a part of my daily routine. When I hadn't made so many friends. When I was completely separate from the world—my postpartum wounds still healing, while the world turned upside down, seemed to right itself, and then swung back to upside down. Those days, it was all about survival: snatch up as much sleep as possible, even if it was just in short fifteen-minute bursts. Try to avoid looking up Worldometer on my phone and try to avoid the terrifying thoughts that crept into my head, especially at 3 a.m. when I was up feeding Bruno and it truly did feel like a new day might never come. Those days were a blur of tasks: Feed the baby. Change the baby. Try to do a number two on the toilet. Feed the baby again and gulp down some food while trying not to spill it on him. Wake up at 11 p.m., 1 a.m., 3 a.m., 5 a.m. and then just give up on any further nighttime sleep. Try to keep myself from falling asleep while feeding him by shopping on eBay. Buy beautiful dresses that will collect dust on the clothes rack that is my wardrobe, because no one—and certainly not me— will be able to do all those ordinary things like going to a cafe for a long while yet. That life, those months of darkness, now feels like it happened to someone else.

After a while, I stretch my arms above my head, my body feeling a little creaky, realizing I've been writing nonstop for an hour even though it feels like only ten minutes have passed. Rays of sun coming in through the window are bathing my feet in gold and heating my whole body. I feel so warm that I get up to open the window. Laughter and chatter and a low hum of a song that I can't quite recognize filter in through the window in a gust. I notice that the old lady is out on her balcony again. She is shaking off a tablecloth—one, two, three shakes and then she starts folding it, with quick agile movements as if she's done this a thousand times before. I wonder what meal she's eaten on that tablecloth and with whom. She places the tablecloth down somewhere behind her and again, as she did this morning, she leans her arms onto her balcony rail and gazes out onto the parking lot. The kids with scooters have long gone, and now the lot is empty. I lean my arms onto the rim of my own window and my head enters the spotlight of the sun's rays. Suddenly the lady turns and looks in my direction. I'm not sure if she can see me but I smile at her.

Today there is a glow in the air that carries the memory of summer, the hope and the faith that it will arrive once again.

Timing

Chana G Miller

Such a whimsical notion:
how a single ray split from the sun
and shot through space and time
just to kiss your sullen forehead
in the exact moment
you first felt complete in your existence.

Sun Head

Sophia Zuo

The sun, above me like a
Yellow showerhead   I step under
Its drops   naked and cold
To feel the soil open up
Before me   like a shudder.
The sun peers on like a
Magnifying glass so
Air becomes static and my body's
Suspended under tempered glass.
I am but   a collection
Of bone dust, my outlines
Made dandelion by day.
Will the sun ever be
Close enough to lick me
Whole?   I hope so.
I want to feel what it feels
To be bathed by pure flame.
I am small, but
The only time I wish I was bigger
Is under the sun.
Only then my body, an indigo well, could hold
Just a morsel more.

White Light

Kris Spencer

In the simplicity of the great white light all color lives.
—Winifred Nicholson

Winifred Nicholson would collect
wildflowers and place them in a jug
for a lamp on a dull day. To a butter-like mass

of blossoms she once added two violet
everlasting peas and saw the yellows
break free like music. Here, we throw

the shutters back. Air rushes in
with the flinty smell of rain, and rasp
of insects and shifting grass. Like light.

Breaking into luminosity: my hands at work,
your shoulder moving as you wake, the roundness
of our baby's heel. Outside, a maple turns

from brown-green to lime-yellow with the passing
of a cloud. Colors split and merge as a rainbow
in a stormy sky. And, the flowers glowing on the table.

Life
Drawing

Kris Spencer

She sits on a pale sofa, distant as landscape; flesh pinked
like sunset by the three-bar heater. The first mark, a point
of sight anchored on the pale paper. For proportion, the bones

scratched in with a blunt tip. Edges recede and merge.
Perspective deceives and wobbles in light and shadow,
changeable as the sea. The charcoal stripes form tunnels

and ladders. Lines scraped down to give breadth, and pushed
across for depth. Muscles mapped with spheres and cylinders
and cones; bulk compressed. An hour to find the color

in another's light. Shadows formed with burnt terra verde
to mold curves and hollows; mixed in with aquamarine to
give an impression of air. For the luminous skin, orange-blue

and yellow-violet in oil pastel; stubbed thin with rag to
make the colors glow. For a moment, I catch the harmony
and dissonance of line, and the melody enclosed. I struggle

to be truthful. Tangled up in the light and shade, my line flies
to other bodies I have known. Vision changes as it observes.
As the light goes, with no mirror to judge what my eyes have

missed or added, I look beyond my drawing and back to the
model lying naked on the couch. In the play of things, I hold
something of the endless meaning which is another's form. Not

truth but some equivalent; a kind of intimacy, unfamiliar and
mute. The slopes and shelves of a body collapsed and redrawn
so that the sum of revisions becomes a whole, for a moment.

Reeled In

Andrea Watson-Canning

Across from the shop was a small fountain. Lee set up so that his view was of the fountain statue and the riotous explosion of colors at the storefront. Aquas and sun-drenched sands, sunsets of lilacs and mauves. It was shocking to see such intimate clothing flaunted so brazenly, hung like laundry drying, or flags celebrating a national holiday.

The fountain was an antiquated bauble—a mermaid astride a dolphin—a rococo monstrosity. The true subject would be the juxtaposition of mermaid and her contemporary grotto—strewn with the clothes she left behind. This was *art*—a perfect example of the irony of contemporary life.

Lee sketched the store—bikinis and thongs tumbling out of baskets as if creeping flowers. Bras hanging from trees, ripe fruit ready to be picked. He turned his attention to the mermaid on the dolphin, her arm raised with conch in hand. Was it freedom or victory? He slowly put his pencil down, contemplating the statue.

His eyes drifted to the shop. There she was, sitting at the counter idly thrumming, a pearl-shimmering teddy behind her framing turquoise hair. He was mesmerized by the angelic effect. An improbable effusion of flowers—lilies, roses, daisies, birds of paradise—sprang from her dress. On her left ear, piercings scaled her lobe and cartilage. She pulled out a brown bag and opened it. She removed a sandwich, a cheese and cracker packet, and a juice box, laying them out on the wrinkled brown bag. She indelicately poked a hole in the juice box and slurped. She unwrapped the sandwich—the smell of tuna wafted his way—and chomped.

A wave of ocean salt and kelp stunned him. Lee began sketching the woman—staring indiscreetly, blindly drawing, etching her features into his mind. He was lost in this vision—a goddess amid the banal.

She slurped the last of the juice, wrapped up her trash, and shoved it into the overfilled can next to the counter. Looking down, she sighed, picked up the garbage, and headed into the back. Then she was gone, shielded by hanging unmentionables.

Lee considered his sketch. Her hair flowed free as if caressed by currents; she meticulously spread cheese on her snack cracker. He stood suddenly, knocking over his chair. Gulls shrieked their indignance. Sketchbook firm in hand, he walked over, sure of his course. He reached the baskets and hangers filled with intimacies, and hesitated. But the smell of seawater and sand lured him in.

The shop was netted with lace and silk. Tables were piled high with jewel-toned fabrics. Satin-soft, tempting him to touch—to caress. Babydoll nighties and delicate peignoirs. He moved deeper into the store, searching. Tables crowded together. Soft and tempting gave way to sensual and thrilling. Silk and satin became fishnet and leather. His heart pounded as he sidled through bustiers and corsets. Soon, he was pushing through racks of hosiery and garter belts, tangling in their straps, caught.

Suddenly, the smell of seawater was close. He looked up, and she was there. Turquoise hair dappled by a cool light as if reflecting a faraway sun. She leaned in, close to his tangled prison, and reached out. Lee thought she might caress his face.

Instead, she untangled his sketchbook from the racks. "You need to be a little more careful with your stuff—this is silk and runs easily."

Her voice was moonlight on tidal waters. Lee swallowed. "I'm, uh, sorry . . . I wasn't paying attention."

She smiled. "Yeah—you bumped into a few of my tables. Is there something you are particularly looking for?"

"Um, yeah . . . I mean, no . . . I . . . don't know?"

Her look was gentle. "First time? It's okay—a lot of people start off with something simple and not too obvious. A neutral-colored bra and panty set is a good bet. Let me show you."

The woman led Lee to a table. "These are my favorites," she said as she delicately fingered the fabric. "Feel this." She offered the panties for his consideration. "The lightly embossed shell pattern is feminine without drawing attention. The material is a kiss on the skin. And the abalone sheen is so pretty when it hits the light."

Lee's pulse quickened. She eyed him appraisingly.

"You're about a 44 chest and 37 waist?" She rifled through the sets. "This one would do. What do you think?"

He gaped, a fish out of water as he took hold of the set. She looked uncertain.

"I have sexier items if you want to try those?" She moved to another table with corsets and other items in garish red and black.

"No! Umm . . . these are . . . fine . . ." Lee's courage failed him.

She walked him to the counter and rang up the purchase. She wrapped the lingerie in perfumed tissue paper and gently placed it in a bag, which she handed over to Lee. It smelled of salt breezes.

The woman smiled sweetly and winked. "When you're ready for something bolder—come on back!" Lee shot out of the store like a life preserver springing to the ocean surface. He ran past the fountain and stopped abruptly. The sketchbook.

Hali watched the man bolt like a colt from her store. She had observed him earlier in the week, his lanky frame hunched over his sketch pad as he drew during the lunch hour. She liked the way he brushed back an unruly lock of brown hair when he looked up. She hoped she hadn't scared him away.

She noticed the sketchbook on the counter. She slid the book over, hesitated for a moment, then opened it. She flipped through sketch after sketch of her store, her figure slight behind a hazy window, but growing larger on each successive page. And then—a gentle portrait of her eating lunch, hair flowing. It was absurd. It was lovely. She closed the book and, cradling it in her arms, she looked out. The man was slowly walking back to her.

sketching the woman

    etching her features

        into his mind

Portrait of an Artist, Bedridden

Maija Haavisto

I want you to draw
a hundred different pictures
of me lying in bed
a hundred different poses and
pretend it's exciting
a hundred different still lifes
like vases with tulips
and bind them together
into a flipbook
so you can bring me to life
frame by frame

I don't want to be a statue
the pores of marble can't breathe
I want those lines to
capture me and release me
I want my unkempt curves
to look elegant and lusty
and to bloom like fiery tulips
I want the pencil lead to snap
because there's so much life
in those lines it doesn't fit
in two-dimensional trees
I want the curators to gasp:
stilled, she still lives

Reunion

Lauren Linkowski

The last time I saw you, I can't remember
why I pretended I would leave
so soon. It seemed like it was that time:
after the coffee, the pie with its stiff veneer
of meringue, coffee again, acrid
then sweet. You said stay. Help me
clean up this mess, save what's left.
The dishes brushed up against each other,
a gentle chatter of ceramic tongues. We talked
about lemons and how they flower all year long,
how hard it can be to have any kind of faith
that the first one you touch is good
inside. You asked how I could be so sure
of what's hidden under the skin:
eternal summer or bitter pith?
What's cut can't open up again.
I shrugged. When you know you know.
Our hands touched under the murky water.
We stood at the window a long time after
we were finished. Silent, we watched
the yellow sun ripen, then drop
from the branches of the darkening sky.

Running

Kristin Celms

The last night I spend with you, we sweat naked on the bed. The breeze coming through the windows is like exhaust from a motor. I watch a bead of perspiration drop from your forehead to the pillow. Your eyes are closed; your finger slides along my arm. Summer in Arezzo, my hair wild and wavy in the atmosphere that presses down like a velvet curtain. I slip from my room and run through the cobbled streets so he won't see me coming to you.

The summer language class was my wish. I've never been outside the Midwest—I have never been anywhere. Mike came along because we're in love, because he wants me to be happy. An adventure. For me it is a blinding light. The world is bigger, older, more beautiful than I imagined. And one day you appear at the university and lead us to the Piero della Francesca frescoes at the Basilica di San Francesco. You pull us along the nave of the church with your words, drawing us to the paintings that cover every surface up to the ceiling. I have never heard a man speak so passionately about art before, expose his emotions without embarrassment. I can't stop looking at the Madonna clothed in blue and red, standing to receive the annunciation from the angel Gabriel. My gaze shifts from the Madonna to your face, glowing with your love of this place. Then I can't stop looking at you.

So much beauty, so much sex, crammed into these weeks. In between, I look out the window of my tiny room near the university, a twin bed and dresser behind me. I look out the window of Mike's room on the floor above, slipping into my sandals. I look out the window of the Bar di Domenico, past the mahogany woodwork, the dark golden walls, watching you wave a cheerful goodbye. I look out the window of your bedroom, panting.

When I was little I imagined I was running ten miles, fifty, one hundred, my feet hitting the sidewalk, the grassy hills in the park, spraying gravel by the swing set. Flying up Mount Olympus in my winged shoes. Euphoria.

This is what being with you is like.

On the airplane, I feel Mike's elbow jostle mine. He doesn't know, I hear inside my head. The air chills me, my fingertips cool to the touch. He wants me to marry him. I want to be a photographer. I sit still, trying not to move my hands, counting down from a hundred ten or twenty times until I have become a shell of a person, just for these hours in the plane, because I don't know how to talk to Mike. I don't want to hurt him. I don't know what my voice will sound like and whether, if I let him look at me straight on, he will see into my soul and find you there.

You think you are an interlude: I enjoyed you during my time in Italy before going back to my old life. You are half right. I come home with the knowledge of you bursting out of my body. That first night, my fingers are clicking on the keys, searching for one-way flights to Pisa. I can't keep my passion in—I call Anna the next day and out it spills.

I open my hand. The tiny glass cat you gave me from Venice. I keep it in my backpack. Sometimes I carry it in the front pocket of my jeans. I have a concrete goal now, resting on the painted clouds of an Italian basilica. I'm almost twenty-two. In ten years, my photos will be in magazines. Photos of the Italy where I live. I'm going to graduate before I go back to you, my parents want me to get my degree. This is my concession to them, my time to catch my breath. I have the rest of my life to be in Italy. It's only ten months.

Ten months is long enough to have sex with eighty-eight guys, a different one each Saturday and Sunday night.

Ten months is long enough to finish Italian Language 2 and 3.

Ten months is long enough for my mother to be diagnosed with cancer and die.

After I've taken dozens of hot showers to scrub the pain off of me, to burn it off; after I spend days and weeks in bed while Mike goes to his new job after graduation; after I open my eyes and draw the curtain back because I want to see the sun, and there's a cardinal sitting in the maple tree calling to her mate and I can hear this sound, I'm not disconnected from the world anymore; after I'm drinking a pinot noir in a wine bar and see a dark-haired man walk by outside, and I'm transported in an instant back to Arezzo running through the streets to get to your front door, running like I'm being chased by lions and I'm standing on the step, hitting the door with my fists, knowing I will die if I don't get in; after that, I write to you. I receive an answer several days later. You're married.

Mike and I stand inside a brick church with copycat stained glass windows and stucco walls to say our vows. I close my eyes to stop comparing this to the basilica in Arezzo. The church doesn't matter anyway. I look at Mike's kind face. A new start. We honeymoon in Hawaii, running as far away as I can get from Europe. We drink rum punch.

When we get back to Minnesota, I stop running. For a short while, time and space collapse. My world is the apartment—pieces of it—the end of the sofa where I sit with her in my lap, the side of the bed where I barely sleep, the glider in her room, the top of the changing table where her legs kick. My little Maddie. The world is small and I burrow in and close the door behind me, I don't want anything else to come in.

A few months later I understand that this was the interlude.

I buy the textbook for a class on Renaissance art that I can't attend, and at night after Maddie's in her crib I set it on my lap and page through. The little glass cat sits on my bedside table next to the picture of my mother. Several photos of the Piero della Francesca frescoes of Arezzo are in the book. Will I ever see you again, I whisper.

The letters begin. My sole form of creative expression. Love letters to you, to Italy, to a world that made me feel more than I ever had before. When I finish each one I save it on my desktop in a folder named Miscellaneous.

Maddie reaches for the glass cat. I tell her no.

I find the photo album I made in a plastic tub in the basement. I took these pictures when I was going to become a photographer, so there are fake-artsy photos of corners of buildings, close-ups of church interiors, chair legs in a bar. Photos of the Piero della Francesca Virgin Mary. None of you. Those I keep in the top drawer of my dresser. The album looks new, untouched. I made it while I was at home with my parents, when I believed I was going back to Italy. I page through it, trying to recapture the feeling.

Maddie opens the cabinet behind our sofa and pulls out a sheaf of printer paper, which she covers with pictures in pencil, marker, acrylic paint. She likes to draw cats, blue cats, red cats, purple cats, fuzzy tails thick like elephant legs. I straighten the pieces of paper so the edges match up and place them on her desk. I wonder if I would have taken art classes in Italy. I wonder if you and I would have painted together.

Mike tells me I can take a class. I appreciate the thought, but he doesn't understand. I'm in this life now. I'd be playing at something that doesn't fit.

I go to the bookstore to find a donation for the charity book drive at Maddie's school and stop to look at the wall of magazines. *Travel + Leisure* has a photograph of the cathedral in Florence on the cover. I head to the travel section where there are three books about planning a trip to Tuscany. One of them has several pages on Arezzo. I buy it.

I have a little shelf now. My art book. My photo album from Italy. The guidebook for Tuscany. My camera. The glass cat.

Today I am thirty-two years old. Maddie gives me a handmade card. More than ten years since my time in Arezzo. If I had gone back, I would be working at my photography of churches, of people reading books and looking at art, photos of the Piero della Francesca frescoes and landscapes, maybe just the edges. I would be wrapped in scarves, with long unkempt hair, a barrette holding one side sloppily back. And you would be there, fixing me an espresso in your golden kitchen.

I hold my phone in front of me, a blank email template on the screen. I type in your address and a few sentences, wait, then hit Send. I don't know if this is still your email address. I don't know what I'm wishing for. In a week I receive an answer. You're no longer married. The words travel through me, tingling in my fingertips, up my back.

Now that I know this, I can't un-know it.

I book the Albergo di Roma. The first place we drank together without Mike. I couldn't stop laughing—we were in Arezzo, in Tuscany, one of the most beautiful places on earth, and this hotel was trying to be like Rome. Did I seem carefree to you? My momentary reaction to a sign on a hotel pressing us together like the seal on a Ziploc bag.

Maddie settles down next to me, pushing a spiral notebook and metal case of colored pencils onto my lap.

"I don't want you to go."

"I know you don't."

"I'm going to draw a picture for you every night. What's your favorite color?" Her fingers find mine.

"Make sure you get to bed on time."

Before I leave, Anna asks if I've thought this through.

"This wasn't what my life was supposed to be."

"If you don't come back, you won't have Maddie anymore, not like you do now."

I chew my lip after saying goodbye.

Compared to the thousands of words I've saved on my desktop addressed to you, the response I've sent is brief. It starts out longer but then I go back and hit Delete over and over again. I'm not sure what to say except that I'm coming and I've missed you. It's a relief that you say you'd like to see me. I'm glad I didn't reveal too much. Yet.

Maddie clutches my arm when I sit up in her bed. Her fingers are tacky—eating that chocolate chip muffin after dinner. How can she brush her teeth, wash her hands, change into pajamas and this stickiness remains like a tattoo. She doesn't want me to leave her bed. I resettle myself beside her. I need to finish packing.

Before I go out the door, Maddie pushes a dense, flat packet into my hand. "It's for you, Mommy," she says. "When you get lonely in Italy."

I slide into my seat. I always choose the aisle. A woman with a blue cardigan over a red T-shirt and an *Oprah* magazine on her lap is by the window. I don't put my seatbelt on because someone might end up sitting between us. I'm going to see you again. I can't stop shivering.

She needs to understand that I deserve to have a life.

My photo album didn't sharpen the accuracy of my memories with all of those close-ups and angles. It's hard for me

---

to match my photos to current-day Arezzo, hard for me to find the chair legs and building corners I snapped pictures of years ago. The Albergo di Roma I remember is eight windows across, its exterior a creamy white, double doors at the front. This one is a dull tan, four windows across, a single door covered in a film of dust. And where is the piazza that I thought we crossed when we walked toward each other? This is on an ordinary narrow street. I have come thousands of miles and lost a night's sleep and I don't recognize a thing.

I stop at the Bar di Domenico. I need a drink. I need something. When I open my purse, I see the rectangular-shaped bundle from Maddie. A handmade envelope. "FOR MOMMY" in purple block letters on the front. I lift the taped flap and pull out the folded sheet of paper. She has drawn two of her cats, a small one curled up against a larger one. Hearts floating across the sky above.

The Basilica di San Francesco is around the corner from the bar. Outside, it's a dull brown structure of rectangular stones, one round window on the gable end of the façade. Inside the stunning frescoes cover the walls. In the cool, still air of the cathedral I experience a jolt of recognition. This, at last, feels familiar. I walk up the aisle looking from frame to frame, starting on the left. When I'm almost to the altar, I see her, clothed in a swirl of a red dress, a blue cape over her shoulders. The Virgin Mary in the Annunciation. She stands almost as tall as the column of her house, her hand up. Accepting the visit from the angel Gabriel, her role as mother of God.

Maddie's drawing a picture for me every night before bedtime. Trying not to feel so far away in the dark.

On the way, a man in sandals crosses in front of me, his brown robe held together with an old leather belt around his waist. I pass a woman in a blue shawl, her red dress reaching to her ankles. I'm no longer in my present, even in my century. I've crossed some border into another world. There's your street, number 24. You're expecting me, you may be standing on the other side of the wall. If that door opens I can change the course of my life, turn it ninety degrees. I watch my hand move to the bell, hear it chime inside. The door opens.

I say you look exactly the same. It isn't true, but it isn't a lie. I still see you. It feels natural to hug you, to let you hug me. You're divorced. I'm in limbo. We're both, in our own ways, available. You stand back so I can move past you into the hall. You take me to the kitchen at the back of the house. I think about the rooms above, your bedroom in the front.

You pour me a glass of wine. I watch while your back is turned. I want to wrap my arms around you again, I want to hold on. You sit down across from me, handing me my glass. You're teaching at the university, still bringing students to the Piero della Francesca frescoes. When you ask about my family, I say they're fine. I'm looking at your hand, flexed around your opposite forearm, the hand that once rested on my thigh in the bedroom upstairs. Can a life become something else entirely, so easily? After all of these years can I say yes and this will become mine?

I can't hold the glass. I set it down. Then my hands are fumbling in my bag, pulling out my wallet. My fingers slide the picture across the table.

There is a long pause. My index and middle fingers are still on the photo, holding her against the worn wooden table.

I raise my eyes, and watch you see me.

"She's beautiful," you say.

You know. Perhaps you knew it all along. If I had been running toward you, you would have seen it on my face.

"She's an artist," I say.

I hadn't noticed.

From the front stoop of the Albergo di Roma, I move in a widening spiral. I eat raspberry gelato the color of Mary's dress. I find a tiny storefront with silk scarves and choose one in deep reds and blues. I pull out my camera and snap photo after photo. A man sitting at a tiny round table with a glass of wine in front of him, stained maroon rings on the white tablecloth. Two children carrying a basket between them filled with tomatoes, lettuce, beans. A woman in a blue dress, calling to her daughter, arm outstretched to clasp the tiny hand.

My life can take a ninety-degree turn without me moving an inch. It's in the perspective.

I'm on hold with Delta Air Lines. There should be an empty seat tomorrow. Maybe even tonight.

Running toward her.

Promise of the World

Laura Ma

to Akshi

We begin with sunlight, flames bursting in gold, souls
burning to completion. From February days, we travel

to March, the solstice eclipsing the world and dipping
winter to its vernal equinox. At the big bang of our

universe, you said I shined with an unreal light, that
whatever I had on the surface was too fake to be true.

Perhaps you saw through the eternal landscape, saw it
cracked and wanted more. Because it is always in the

midst of the start, when the shadows are the darkest,
when all good stories begin. This is the genesis: the

fate of our collision, our warmth. A bush of yellow
roses waiting in silence. For it begins in winter, flames

barely flickering through the crevices of broken palms,
fingertips alight with hidden gold. Frost covers my blistered

palmistry, gilded smiles sheening in brilliance. You
have the hands of a healer: the sun child, the flaring divine.

They guide me, hold me, unearth me. *Do you believe
in forever?* You are the transition, my final destination.

I want to return to a new home with you, glittering with
mirrors that refract unveiled memories. I am in love with

your happiness, in love with every laced hand, in love
with every murmured good night. Laurels woven with golden

petals in full bloom: *This is what we want and this is who we'll be.*

Because it is always in the midst of the start, when the shadows are the darkest, when all good stories begin.

The Robins Build Their Nests in Spring and So Did We

Olivia Landry

I waited all winter to be with you. Until then, we made shrimp pasta in your kitchen in the dark at 4:30 p.m. We went for snowy walks in layers of mittens and scarves around your subdivision. I saw a mirror on the ground and tried to take our picture in it, but by the time I'd wrestled off one of my gloves our reflection was too covered in snow to be recognizable. Over the winter break, we watched every Marvel movie, sometimes watching two or three a day so that we would finish them all by early January. We felt like we were passing time until we could really be together—not just on weekends, not just when the snow wasn't too bad. When spring came, it was a spring like I had never seen. I touched crocuses on strangers' lawns to make sure I wasn't just imagining them. I watched robins hop across mucky fields ripping worms out of the ground with a fierce sense of purpose. I saw buds on trees bloom and knew *this was it*. By mid-April I had handed in my resignation and we were looking at apartments. In the warmth of May we sat across from each other, feet nearly touching, in our new 489-square-foot home. Our parents knew *this was it* and turned our bedrooms into rest stops for guests. People cautioned us about living together before marriage, that we'd *ruin the magic* of it all but we didn't listen. It was a spring like we had never seen, and nothing would be the same again.

Leave the Light On

Olivia Landry

Spring came.
You found me
like you always do,
and we built a world together
where we could finally breathe.

love as layers of the atmosphere

n. m. letscher

Content warning: self-harm, suicidal thoughts

"I feel like I'm dreaming," they say, almost whispering into her chest, listening to the sound of her breathing.

Perhaps you are, is not what she says back. They cannot help the small tears that gather briefly in the corner of their eyes (cumulonimbus), even as they coincide with a smile. These too-soon droplets are quickly blinked away.

"Kiss me again?" they ask.

She does.

Outside the panes of sleep, the sun is rising even as it rains.

The bed is warm when they wake, but she isn't there.

Outside, the sky is gray. There aren't cloud types here. Everything inside is refreezing, dying if they're being dramatic, numbing if they're being honest.

"Are you okay?" she asks.

"I'm not. But I will be," they answer.

They fall apart and slowly put the pieces back together, staring toward the horizon. Just past the gray-white of the clouds (altostratus), there is blue; beyond that, all the stars of the universe. A small zephyr and they'd thin. They know this.

It would be easier, they whisper to themself, *to crawl into the snow and sleep 'til spring.*

Outside it is snowing.

Across the city, they are watching the snow fall in the streetlights. It is the dry kind, the kind that glints and sparkles eerily and beautifully at the same time. This is the third time this week it has snowed (nimbostratus). They whisper a wish just for themself.

The bed is empty. It always is.

Their mouth is open, stretched in a silent scream because everything hurts, and everything is wrong, and they don't even feel real. No one is to know about this, or how it keeps happening. Thunderstorm after thunderstorm, with thunder and lightning spectacular enough to split a skull, but not enough to quench a brain on fire.

There should be a certain irony to their breaking down in the shower of all places over others, but that's not important right now.

The important thing is the half-moon crescents (cirrocumulus) on their right forearm, which they know will fade, but from which they also know that they were hoping to draw blood. The worst thing is that they don't really know when these half-moon crescents will feel necessary.

They wrap their arms around themself, around knees and rib cage as the sobs come rushing back. They've lost count of how many times now. Their hands run over arms, spine, face, trying to feel corporeal, tangible, real, not steam (stratus) or smoke.

The thing is, though, that they always have a part of them that is cataloging experiences for later. Always for later. Especially when now and then are much more painful. They contain the clouds long enough to crawl into their too-empty bed. Admitting is for the morning. Tonight, they are falling apart, and then.

Then they will tell about it.

The world warms. To them, it seems impossible for a bit, but then they realize that it is how it works. The devil's in the details, but each breath of soft, misty green across branches is a welcome, petrichor-scented warmth (cirrus to cirrostratus).

There are still moments when the world fractures, but they keep a hold of themself.

They imagine kisses. The soft shush of sheets in the twilight of the tail end of a thunderstorm. Names like gemstones. Stars and galaxies and sparks. Always on their mind, at the base of their skull.

They imagine the future like the sun peeking through clouds.

They make dinner together. Light a candle after it is over and the dishes are washing, like a soft tide from the kitchen.

They put on music and hold out their hand. She takes it, pulls them in close. The music is older than the two of them combined.

"Do you want me to lead?" they ask.

"Want is different than letting," she says, the hint of laughter like a ray through the clouds (altocumulus).

"Alright, will you let me lead?" they ask, laughing slightly and half rolling their eyes.

"For now."

The two dance, and it is all there is, for a time. Eventually, the music is over and they are both swaying as the record softly spins, and the lightest of droplets hit the glass and skitter down.

"It's almost time to wake up," she says, tilting their head up by the chin.

"But I don't want to. You won't be there with me," they say, still holding onto her. "You never are."

She smiles, brows gathering briefly like a line of storm clouds (stratocumulus) before clearing. She kisses them once, and then pulls back.

"Try me."

Their eyes slowly blink open, the red of behind the lids becoming the glory of the sun.

"Good morning," they hear her say, from behind them, head propped up on one hand, elbow resting on the pillow. A future, a day and longer (cumulus), in two words.

"Good morning," they say back, smiling 'til the ice melts.

It is a beautiful day.

They imagine the future like the sun peeking through clouds.

outer spaces

Kaitlan Bui

suppose this clumsy body, which i call mine,
was also intimately yours, suppose we
were able to put into words the way
the naked sun, fumbling into something
called life, unravels to
a woman.

and suppose the broken door, eased forward,
was more a call to entrance than anything else,
and there was no fear, is no fear,
in walking unaccompanied,
unlonelied by the darkness.

suppose we love in the outer spaces
of our bodies, and plant pearls in the beds
of our starcrossed, sunwashed bones, and suppose we
wake up to the call of the moon, her blemishes
unabashed.

suppose the moon were unabashed.
suppose we, you, i
are, too.

We've Only Met Once Before (On a Different Planet)

Jo Matsaeff

In my hometown the sky always goes from blue to white to gray,
slowly announcing *the rain is coming,* kind enough
to leave people the time to find shelter

or grab the raincoat asleep at the bottom of their bag.
Here in Brussels the sky goes straight from white to wet
doesn't wait for the sun's act to be finished to steal the show

and all of a sudden I'm running in a city I don't know.
Back when I was a kid I once told my mum *If it starts raining*
in a movie you know something big is about to happen.

And this is big, as big as my fear of coming here in the first place.
Bigger than capital cities, bigger than forgotten luggage
on the subway that make all the alarms in my brain go off,

bigger than all the maps I can't read, bigger than the version of me
from last year who thought sweetness was over.
The rain is faster than us, we can't escape it

and now here I am drenched in possibilities,
soaked in realization that amazing things
can still happen to me.

You took me to a forest I never knew existed, and when
I told you I also had social anxiety you said *I know,*
that's how we met, remember?

For the first time I thought *what a beautiful thing
to be that scared of people if it means
you can meet the right ones.*

You were the last stranger I got to meet before the pandemic,
my last scary party, last protest before everything in the world
and in my family turned grayer than the sky,

my last raised fist in the middle of a happy song.
And here you are, a year and a half later. Still existing,
so real I can actually touch your hand, so beautiful it's okay

to hug you. A proof yesterday is still dancing somewhere, eyes shut,
oblivious to the fact that tomorrow is here.
A few years ago in another poem to another boy I said

I'm always holding an imaginary umbrella above your head
but this time I'm throwing the umbrella away,
I want us as exposed and alive as can be.

This time I press pause and we keep running through
a frozen city, all the raindrops up in the air, waiting, just like me,
hoping this free fall will last forever.

That somewhere in the process the ground ceased to exist,
that crashing only happens in real life now.
When we finally collapse on the bench of a bus shelter,

you look at your feet and apologize for the rain.
And I've never met someone as unaware
of their own beauty. I laugh to make you feel better.

Come on, you're not important enough to make it rain.
I hope you don't mind but just for a minute
I make a baby with you in my head.

This baby grows up as fast as I fall for you and turns into a kid
with a head full of questions so when they ask me when I first knew
I had a crush on you

I just point at the bus stop and say *There, right there.*
Maybe humans are not important enough
to make it rain

but still, when I watch you dance through the small window
of my phone the next day a hundred tiny clouds
come bursting on the edge of my eyes.

Purple Lipstick

Jo Matsaeff

I ordered my purple lipstick online.
It came a few weeks later in a brown envelope
with *queerness* written in invisible ink all over it.
I locked my bedroom door and unwrapped it

like a secret, both feverish and careful
with a lot of *maybes*. The same way I'd confessed
to my boyfriend a few days before that I kind of wanted
to date women and I wasn't really sure I was one myself.

He'd hugged me with hands that already meant nothing,
he'd explained how we would get through this
together. Inside my head a thousand purple mouths
shouting *How do you get through what you're supposed to be?*

So I waited for a few weeks, learned how to use
my purple weapon quietly, in the safety of my own mirror.
It was so different from the red one I used to apply messily as a kid.
It's not that I don't like red lipstick
but that I only like it on other people,

just like my birth name. I became obsessed with purple,
so neutral and daring at the same time. I started wearing it
outside the house and my new friends told me my face
was so much more colorful with a smile on it.

So one day I left, packed all my things,
nearly leaving my lipstick behind on the sink
for the one who would come after me but
I grabbed it at the last minute

to leave one more message to my past self
on the mirror and threw it in my purple backpack
along with the rest of my dreams, hoping they
would make more sense under a different roof.

I was wearing it the day I moved into a shared house
with a rainbow on the door and to my first Pride,
to my first open mic, to a thousand first times
of feeling like myself.

It's been sleeping at the bottom of a drawer these days
with the rest of my makeup. But I still wear it,
on days like today or whenever I need
to remember what freedom tastes like.

a thousand first times of feeling like myself

Leaving the Woods

Elizabeth Wittenberg

Our sunsets here are numbered now.

Of course the sun will continue to set when we leave,
set in the same way in these same places that we've seen it,

but will we

slow down every day at this time
right before we sleep
(quickly & deep-solid)
and simply watch
with reverence as
the sun slides downward
colors layering behind the
silhouette of pines?

Our sunsets and our sunrises and our nights under the stars
like this are numbered
and we will never get them back.

They will live on in
lackluster photos & golden-hued memories,
but we will never get them back.

I remind myself to continue
stopping
to breathe, think, blink,
and appreciate this

spectacularly beautiful world

and the freedom I have in living
this life that is entirely mine
and entirely for me.

of course the sun
will continue to set
when we leave

Potential Energy

Elizabeth Wittenberg

I have had a beautiful year
without you in it

but sometimes the taste
of my own mouth

makes me miss you
in some small and shameful corners

of my heart and mind and soul
I don't hate you

but

I was half-alive before you left me
and I didn't even know

I did not understand that
the good part I was waiting for

the whole damn time
was who I'd be without you

Ever Again

Jessica Barksdale

The happiest days of her marriage to Henry were the four months she spent in Florence without him. One spring semester of marital bliss, Alice teaching in Italy, Henry in San Francisco, working his nine-to-five in a glass building downtown. Unlike when they were together, her stomach prickled with excitement when she saw his face, her throat sparkling with all she wanted to tell him over WhatsApp.

Henry, too, seemed happy to hear from her, a contrast to the shrugs and the baleful looks he usually threw her when she knocked on his home office door, his expression stuck in a perpetual "What now?"

"I called the gutter guys," Henry said, excited about home improvement projects. "All those maple seed pods. I'm afraid of a flood."

"The students get drunk almost every night," Alice said, after a pause. "But they show up to class."

Behind their conversation, Alice heard the squawk of a Steller's jay.

"I swear the people they are hiring," Henry said. She wondered if he was looking at the clock on their mantel. "Their hair stands up straight, and their glasses are huge. I'm not sure they know what a database is."

"I love you," Alice said when there was nothing left.

"I love you, t—" Henry said, ending the call each time before finishing the sentence.

"See you soo—"

"Fly saf—"

"Henry?" she always said, though he was gone.

In May, Alice returned home, carrying the hope their phone calls had given her. He'd offered to pick her up at the airport, but Alice declined, knowing that the long drive through traffic on 101 would ruin any chance of a happy homecoming. So she rode BART from SFO with her two enormous suitcases filled with crumbling biscotti and bottles of sour Tuscan wine. The skyline had risen since she left, everything in sharp, colorless lines. Henry opened the door, his smile as tight as the skyscrapers.

They lasted two weeks before Henry moved out, taking their cat Louise.

Who takes the cat? Didn't people leave the obligations behind? Houses, children, pets? The cold air sliced in through the old windows, fog trickling in between the cracks. Alice slowly unpacked. She turned in her grades. She flicked through Instagram, watching her students, some still in Europe, still drunk. They were all so young, and all of them—even the awkward, lumpy ones—fresh and beautiful. She was lumpy but old and needed a haircut.

"You've never even mentioned me on Facebook," her stylist Nathan said when she finally got an appointment. It was a last-minute cancellation, and he'd given her dirty hair his perfected withering sneer. "You could have written, 'I can't wait for Nathan to cut this god-awful mess on my head.'"

Alice shrugged. She didn't have enough energy to tell Nathan about Henry. Or Italy.

"Just cut it off." She stared at the mirror, her fatigue a portrait: middle-aged woman in sorrow. "Most of it, at least."

Later, she hoped she looked like some form of Audrey Hepburn, but she was more Dame Judi Dench. Recent Judi Dench. Lovely but recent Judi Dench, a face held together by wrinkles and makeup. Alice went to Safeway and bought popcorn and bananas. She sat in her condo and listened to sirens.

"Why didn't it work?" she'd asked Henry the night he left.

"It worked until it didn't." He zipped his duffle, closed

his suitcase, and slipped his phone into his coat pocket. He picked up the cat carrier, and Alice looked away from Louise's yellow eyes.

But had it? They had no children and owned nothing together, this condo on Potrero Hill an inheritance from her Uncle Ray. They each bought their own cars. They divided up the bills as if they were dealing cards. Electric for you, water for me. Splitzees on the insurance.

In July, Alice filed her retirement papers. Her bright and shiny realtor Kip put the condo on the scorching hot market. For a couple of weeks, she scoured Redfin as if on drugs, clicking and scrolling and scribbling down addresses. Where could she move? What house would she buy? Where would she live her best life?

One night, she fell asleep, real estate site on, waking to a memory. They'd been coming back from Cinque Terre, the bus leaving the highway and taking them into the historic district. The spring sunset stretched gold and then orange against the horizon, brilliant against the warm stone buildings stacked like blocks along the Arno. The students were singing a song Alice had never heard and would not recognize now. Their voices were full of joy but so loud, passersby on the sidewalk looked up at the bus and smiled. Everything glowed, and Alice thought, I will never be in this particular bus with these people. This sun will never be warming the side of my face in this exact way. I will never hear these notes ever again.

Alice's heart had throbbed with the fading sun and the music. Her students' impossible young and smooth and perfect bodies swayed. Watching them had been like being on acid or at least Benadryl. Out of this world. On the sidewalk, people clapped.

She flicked off her computer and headed to the shower, taking time to wash and dry her hair, doing nothing she promised Nathan she would—no product, no round brush, no gel. Then she began packing what the movers hadn't put into the PODS storage unit. She bought a ticket online and took BART back to SFO. Her entire body broke into music only she could hear. Alice looked at the commuters. The boy with the earphones. The woman clutching the paper bag. The man with the briefcase pressed to his chest. She closed her eyes and breathed in the tight human smell as they hurtled forward.

everything glowed

Escape

Karen Lea Armstrong

The dog took off again

Looked back with glinting eyes
then bolted
to the woods, where roots and melting snow (in May)
and burr-bushes, branch-tangles
hindered all pursuit.
We called, cajoled
sent angry words into the wind
which tossed back raven laughter.

Hours later
she appeared gasping, foaming
soaked and reeking
tail trailing spruce and pine
she quivered, lay submissive
                              but
there was no remorse.
She smiled
post wet and woodsy liberation

Smiled.

And we
when did we last run away?
when did
we
last run away?

Abandon this monotonous trail
take my hand, we'll jump the creek and go
racing, rushing
toward the untold promise

joyful

reckless

immune to every plea for our return

*racing, rushing toward
the untold promise*

Contributors

Karen Lea Armstrong is a writer and family physician living in Timmins, Ontario. Her fiction has been published in *Ars Medica* and The Nub: Indie Arts Hub app and nonfiction in *Triathlon Magazine Canada* and *Canadian Family Physician*. In her non-medical, non-writing time, she works to rid the world of misplaced apostrophes and attempts to train her rescue dog to come when called.

Jessica Barksdale is the author of the poetry collection *Grim Honey* and the novel *The Play's the Thing*, both published in 2021. Her novel *What the Moon Did* will be published in February 2023. Recently retired, she taught composition, literature, and creative writing at Diablo Valley College in Pleasant Hill, California, for thirty-two years and continues to teach novel writing online for UCLA Extension and in the online MFA program for Southern New Hampshire University. She lives in the Pacific Northwest with her husband.

V. Bray has been a writer since childhood and still has a box filled with her first "books," usually illustrated with markers and bound with yarn. She writes in many genres, including speculative and historical fiction and poetry. Her work has been published in *About Place Journal*, *borrowed solace*, the anthology *Growing Up Lifespan*, and *The Writer* magazine. Learn more at authorvbray.com.

Kaitlan Bui is studying English and East Asian studies at Brown University, among other things. She writes regularly for *Cornerstone Magazine* and *Post- Magazine*, and her work has been featured by DVAN, *Spellbinder*, and *Kalopsia Literary Journal*.

Andrew J. Calis is a Palestinian American poet, teacher, husband, and father of four. His first book of poetry, *Pilgrimages* (Wipf and Stock, 2020), was praised by James Matthew Wilson for having "the intensity of Hopkins" and for "layer[ing] light on light in hopes of helping us to see." His work has been published in *America, Dappled Things, St. Katherine Review, Presence, Convivium,* and elsewhere. He teaches at Archbishop Spalding High School in Maryland.

Kristin Celms lives in Minnesota with her husband, the younger of her two children, a golden retriever, and several cats. She maintains a large collection of pink sweaters and is currently revising a cozy mystery.

Jeremy Chu is a twenty-five-year-old Filipino Chinese poet, writing as a guest on the unceded territories of the Squamish, Tsleil-Waututh, and Musqueam nations. Chu's work considers how diasporas imprint themselves within the terrains of Western Canada and how fleeting experiences can give presence and tangibility to minority communities.

Jessica Coles (she/her) is a poet and editor from Edmonton, Alberta, Canada (Treaty 6 territory), where she lives with her family and a judgmental tuxedo cat. Her work has appeared in *Prairie Fire, Moist Poetry Journal, Crow Name* (forthcoming), and *You Are a Flower Growing off the Side of a Cliff: A Chapbook about Mental Health and Resiliency.* Her first chapbook, *unless you're willing to evaporate,* is available through Prairie Vixen Press at prairievixenpress.ca.

Sara Davis is a recovering academic and marketing writer who lives in Philadelphia with two elderly cats. Her PhD in

---

American literature is from Temple University. She has previously published flash in *Capsule Stories*, *Cleaver Magazine*, and *CRAFT* literary magazine. She blogs about books and climate anxiety at literarysara.net. You can find her at @LiterarySara.

Luciana Francis is a Brazilian-born, UK-based writer of poetry, fiction, and nonfiction. She holds a BA (hons) in anthropology and media from Goldsmiths, University of London. Her writing has appeared in various publications in print and online, including *Literary Mama*, *Minerva Rising*, *Burningword Literary Journal*, among others; further work is forthcoming in *Cōnfingō Magazine* and *Consilience*. She has recently been nominated for the Pushcart Prize and Best Small Fictions.

Maija Haavisto has had two poetry collections published in Finland: *Raskas vesi* (Aviador, 2018) and *Hopeatee* (Oppian, 2020). In English, her poetry has appeared or is forthcoming in *Wondrous Real*, *ShabdAaweg Review*, *The North*, *Anomaly*, *Asylum*, *Eye to the Telescope*, *Shoreline of Infinity*, and *Kaleidoscope*. You can find her on Twitter at @DiamonDie.

Olivia Landry (she/her) lives in Halifax, Nova Scotia, Canada, and hopes to be a teacher and a writer. She holds a BA in women's and gender studies and an MA in gender studies. She adores her family, friends, and partner and is so thankful that they enjoy reading her poems and stories. You can find her on Instagram at @golden__liv.

Virginia Laurie is an English major at Washington and Lee University whose work has been published in *LandLocked*, *Phantom Kangaroo*, *Cathexis Northwest Press*, and more. You can find her online at virginialaurie.com.

n. m. letscher (they/he) is a genderfluid nonbinary writer from Chicago, Illinois. They have a strong connection to their hometown and feel as though growing up in such a vibrant city has shaped him incredibly in terms of writing, as well as other aspects of their life. He is a recent graduate of St. Olaf College, with a BA in English and theater, with a focus toward dramaturgy. While they love poetry, they also have a strong love for fantasy and science fiction, especially if it has queer representation in it. He has previously been published in *Hypertext Magazine*, *GLITCHWORDS*, and *Capsule Stories*.

Lauren Linkowski (she/they) is a medical education learning specialist with an EdD in higher education. Her professional interests include teaching, learning, and how our brains can be allies or enemies depending on the situation. You can follow her passion for hiking on Instagram at @outsidelink. She lives in the beautiful New York metro area with her supportive partner and less-supportive cat.

Eileen Lynch is a writer and seeker of warm spots to work (/nap) and is probably trying really hard not to put an unnecessary dragon in whatever she's working on at the moment. If you're interested in seeing where her writing ends up next, you can find her at @eileenpdf on Twitter.

Laura Ma (she/her) is a young writer from California. Her work appears or is forthcoming in the *Pollux Journal*, *The Lumiere Review*, *The Aurora Journal*, and elsewhere. At midnight you can find her exploring aesthetics and wishing that it would rain. Find her on Twitter at @goldenhr3.

Jo Matsaeff is a neurodivergent queer teacher based in France. They can be found at their local open mic or virtually hanging out with their international poet friends wishing for a day when a magical tunnel will bring them all together. Their work appears in *Gnashing Teeth Publishing*, *Anti-Heroin Chic*, *Horse Egg Literary*, *The Adriatic*, and *Serotonin*. You can follow them on Instagram at @jo_pangolin.

Chana G Miller (she/her) grew up in Fairbanks, Alaska, but now lives in Ireland. Her work can be found in *ROPES Literary Journal*, *Into the Void*, the *Lucky Jefferson* 365 Collection, *Rejection Letters*, and *Sublunary Review*. She has recently completed her degree at NUI Galway and is working on her debut novel.

Matthew Miller teaches social studies, swings tennis rackets, and writes poetry—all hoping to create home. He and his wife live beside a dilapidating orchard in Indiana, where he tries to shape dead trees into playhouses for his four boys. His poetry has been featured in *Whale Road Review*, *EcoTheo Review*, *River Mouth Review*, and *Ekstasis Magazine.*

Veronica Nation is a Colorado poet and artist whose work can be seen in *Levitate Magazine*, *300 Days of Sun*, *Sink Hollow*, and others. When she is not writing, Veronica enjoys drinking iced coffee, meditating, and reading an assortment of books. You can follow her on Instagram at @rainandpoetry and on her website at veronicanation.com.

Kris Spencer has written seven books. His poems have been published internationally, most recently in *Acumen, Black Fox*

Literary Magazine, The Orchards Poetry Journal, Fenland Poetry Journal, BALLOONS Lit. Journal, Nailpolish Stories, Bluepepper, Briefly Write, and *Allegro Poetry Magazine.* A fellow of the Royal Geographical Society, he often explores landscape and sense of place in his work. He is a head teacher living and working in West London.

Annie Powell Stone (she/her) is a fan of peanut butter toast. Poetry has come back to her after many years away and absolutely saved her sanity during lockdown. Her work has appeared in *Capsule Stories* and *Door Is a Jar,* among others. She lives on the ancestral land of the Piscataway people in Baltimore City, Maryland, with her husband and two kiddos. Read more of her poetry on Instagram at @anniepowellstone.

Andrea Watson-Canning received her MFA in dramaturgy from UC San Diego, worked in the theater for a while, and then somehow became a teacher. Her first piece was published in *The Dillydoun Review.* She lives in Florida with her partner, Bill; daughter, Fiona; and some dogs and cats to keep it interesting.

Elizabeth Wittenberg is a New Orleans-based writer originally from Chicago. When she is not writing, she prefers to be outside and to be moving. She lives for experiences and stories.

Simone Woods is a scientist (re)turned writer who is originally from Australia but currently resides in Munich, Germany. She writes a healthy mix of creative nonfiction, personal essays, and nonfiction articles. You can read more of her writing on her blog lifeinspirationfile.com. When she is not writing, or taking thousands of photos of her sons or the sky, you can find her snuggled up on a chair reading a book.

Hantian Zhang is a writer living in San Francisco. He is a data scientist by day.

Sophia Zuo is a poet based in Taiwan who lived most of her life in New York and was born to two immigrant parents. Her poetry strongly focuses on identity, emotion, and everything in between. In her free time, she likes reading modern lit and listening to good music.

Editorial Staff

Natasha Lioe, Founder and Publisher

Natasha Lioe graduated with a BA in narrative studies from University of Southern California. She's always had an affinity for words and stories and emotions. Her work has appeared in *Adsum Literary Magazine*, and she won the Edward B. Moses Creative Writing Competition in 2016. Her greatest strength is finding and focusing the pathos in an otherwise cold world, and she hopes to help humans tell their unique, compelling stories.

Carolina VonKampen, Publisher and Editor in Chief

Carolina VonKampen graduated with a BA in English and history and completed the University of Chicago's editing certificate program. She is available for hire as a freelance copyeditor and book designer. For more information on her freelance work, visit carolinavonkampen.com. Her writing has appeared in *So to Speak*'s blog, *FIVE:2:ONE*'s #thesideshow, *Moonchild Magazine*, and *Déraciné Magazine*. Her short story "Logan Paul Is Dead" was nominated by *Dream Pop Journal* for the 2018 Best of the Net. She tweets about editing at @carolinamarie_v and talks about books she's reading on Instagram at @carolinamariereads.

Stephanie Coley, Reader

Stephanie Coley is a country girl from Gering, Nebraska. She graduated in 2016 from Concordia University, Nebraska with a BA in English and a minor in art. She has been a journalism teacher, janitor, data technician, and more. Stephanie is a published poet, appearing in the National Creativity Series of 2009 and *Mango* Issue 3, Respeto, in 2017. She is also a winner of the 2020 Historic Posters Reimagined Project, which can be found at the Nebraska History Museum in Lincoln, Nebraska. Stephanie currently works as the program manager at the West Nebraska Arts Center in Scottsbluff, Nebraska. Stephanie joined *Capsule Stories* as a reader in January 2021.

Rhea Dhanbhoora, Reader

Rhea Dhanbhoora worked for close to a decade as an editor and writer before quitting her job and moving to New York to get her master's degree and finally writing the stories everyone told her no one would ever read. Her debut poetry collection, *Sandalwood-Scented Skeletons*, is forthcoming from Finishing Line Press in 2022. Her work has appeared or is forthcoming in publications such as *Sparkle & Blink*, *Awakened Voices*, *Five on the Fifth*, *Capsule Stories Autumn 2020 Edition*, *Fly on the Wall Press*, *HerStry*, *Artsy*, *Broccoli Mag*, and *JMWW*. Her work has been nominated for a Pushcart Prize and Best American Essays. She is currently on the board of directors for the literary organization Quiet Lightning and editor of RealBrownTalk. Rhea joined *Capsule Stories* as a reader in January 2021. She's working on several projects, including a linked story collection about women based in the underrepresented Parsi Zoroastrian diaspora. You can read her work online at rheadhanbhoora.com.

Hannah Fortna, Reader

Hannah Fortna graduated in 2016 from Concordia University, Nebraska, combining her passion for the written word and her affinity for art making with a degree in English and a minor in photography. After a three-year career as a freelance copyeditor, she heard traveling calling her name and now works seasonal jobs in places connected to America's national parks. When she's not selling souvenirs to tourists in gift shops, she enjoys hiking, photographing natural spaces, and writing about the flora and fauna she saw while on the trail.

She reads anything from poetry to middle-grade novels, but the nature-inspired creative nonfiction section is her haunt in any bookstore. Her poetry has previously appeared in *Moonchild Magazine* and *Capsule Stories Spring 2019 Edition*. Hannah joined *Capsule Stories* as a reader in November 2020.

Kendra Nuttall, Reader

Kendra Nuttall is a copywriter by day and poet by night. She has a BA in English with an emphasis in creative writing from Utah Valley University. Her work has previously appeared in *Spectrum*, *Capsule Stories*, *Chiron Review*, and *What Rough Beast*, as well as various other journals and anthologies. She is the author of the poetry collection *A Statistical Study of Randomness* (Finishing Line Press, 2021) and *Our Bones Ache Together* (FlowerSong Press, forthcoming). Kendra lives in Utah with her husband and poodle. When she's not writing, you can find her hiking, watching reality TV, or attempting to pet every animal she sees. You can find out more about her work at kendranuttall.com. Kendra joined *Capsule Stories* as a reader in January 2021.

Rachel Skelton, Reader

Rachel Skelton graduated from William Woods University with a BA in English, a concentration in writing, and a secondary major in business administration, a concentration in management. She has interned for Dzanc Books and now works as a freelance fiction editor specializing in speculative fiction. You can find more information about her work at theeditingskeleton.com. She occasionally tweets about editing at @EditingSkeleton and talks about books she's reading at @TheReadingSkeleton on Instagram. When she's not doing anything reading-related, she's hanging out with her cats, collecting houseplants, and attempting to learn how to crochet. Rachel joined *Capsule Stories* as a reader in January 2021.

Deanne Sleet, Reader

Deanne Sleet is a graduate of Saint Louis University with a BA in English, a concentration in creative writing, and minors in African American studies and women's and gender studies. She has interned for *River Styx* and Midwest Artist Project Services, where she gained experience with grant writing, editing, and writing copy. She is currently the leasing and marketing manager at City Lofts on Laclede and holds the secretary position for SLU's Black Alumni Association. She writes short fiction and poetry, and a novel is in the making. In her spare time, she hangs out with her cat and roller-skates. Deanne joined *Capsule Stories* as a reader in February 2021.

Claire Taylor, Reader

Claire Taylor is a writer in Baltimore, Maryland, where she lives with her husband, son, a bossy old cat, and an anxious dog who longs to be the cat's best friend. Claire's writing has appeared in a variety of publications, and she was a finalist for the 2020 Lascaux Prize in Poetry and winner of the 2021 *Serotonin* New Year's Day poetry competition. Her micro-chapbook, *A History of Rats*, is available from Ghost City Press. Claire is the founder and editor in chief of *Little Thoughts Press*, a print literary magazine of writing for and by kids. Claire joined *Capsule Stories* as a reader in March 2021. A selection of Claire's work is available online at clairemtaylor.com.

Submission Guidelines

Capsule Stories **is a print literary magazine** published once every season. Our first issue was published on March 1, 2019, and we accept submissions year-round.

Become published in a literary magazine run by like-minded people. We have a penchant for pretty words, an affinity to the melancholy, and an undeniably time-ful aura. We believe that stories exist in a specific moment, and that that moment is what makes those stories unique.

What we're really looking for are stories that can touch the heart. Stories that come from the heart. Stories about love, identity, the self, the world, the human condition. Stories that show what living in this world as the human you are is like.

We accept short stories, poems, and remarkably written essays. For short stories and essays, we're interested in pieces under 3,000 words. You may include up to five poems in a single poetry submission (please send them all in one Word document), and only send one story or essay at a time. Please send previously unpublished work only ("published" includes pieces that have been posted or made publicly available on a blog, website, or social media platform). You may only submit one submission per edition. Simultaneous submissions are okay, but please let us know if your submission is accepted elsewhere. Please include a brief third-person bio with your submission, and attach your submissions in a Word document (no PDFs unless your poetry has very specific formatting, please!).

Find our full submission guidelines and current theme descriptions at capsulestories.com/submissions.

Connect with us!
capsulestories.com
@CapsuleStories on Twitter and Facebook
@CapsuleStoriesMag on Instagram

www.ingramcontent.com/pod-product-compliance
Lightning Source LLC
Chambersburg PA
CBHW040533170726
48295CB00012B/456